JAMES McNEILL
WHISTLER

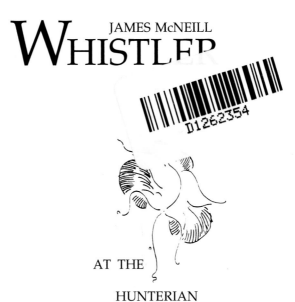

D1262354

AT THE

HUNTERIAN

ART

GALLERY

AN ILLUSTRATED GUIDE

Published with the aid of funds from
The Hugh Fraser Foundation

 The Gallery's 1990 programme is supported
with funds from Glasgow District Council's Festivals Budget

Whistler in his Fulham Road Studio c. 1886

ACKNOWLEDGEMENTS

Since Miss Rosalind Birnie Philip's generous initiative in presenting the University of Glasgow with a representative selection of Whistler's art in 1935, considerable use has been made of the collection, which has been extensively exhibited, researched and published. There has however, been no general guide to the estate, and we trust that this booklet will go some way to satisfying the demand of visitors who, hitherto, have been disappointed to have no souvenir of this remarkable collection.

The booklet forms one contribution to *Glasgow 1990: European City of Culture,* and has been published to coincide with another, *Whistler in Europe,* an exhibition drawn entirely from the University's collection which surveys, for the first time, this American painter's life-long artistic engagement with the Continent.

The preparation of that exhibition, and of this guide, has been the work of Martin Hopkinson, Curator of Prints and Non-Scottish Art. He has received invaluable help from Mrs Margaret MacDonald, Honorary Research Fellow of the Hunterian Art Gallery, and Dr Nigel Thorp, of the University Library's Department of Special Collections. For their scholarship in matters relating to Whistler the Gallery has had good reason to be grateful for many years.

Unless otherwise credited, all photography has been undertaken by Trevor Graham and the staff of the University's Photographic Unit, while typesetting and design have been undertaken by the secretarial and technical staff of the Gallery, in particular June Barrie and Stephen Perry.

Our aim has been to produce a guide for the public to encourage a widening general knowledge of the estate of Whistler for which the University of Glasgow is so fortunate to care. Substantial help has been received towards this aim through generous funding from The Hugh Fraser Foundation, to which body we are deeply grateful. We owe an equal debt of gratitude to Glasgow District Council which has, through its Festivals Office, channelled financial support both towards this publication and many other aspects of the Gallery's 1990 programme.

CHRISTOPHER ALLAN
DEPUTY DIRECTOR

Rosalind Birnie Philip c. 1903

The Hunterian Art Gallery, University of Glasgow, is one of the two principal galleries where a very substantial collection of the work of James Abbott McNeill Whistler (1834-1903) is on view. Its holdings are only rivalled by those of the Freer Gallery of Art, Washington, D.C., U.S.A. This good fortune of the University is principally due to the gift in 1935 and bequest in 1958 by Rosalind Birnie Philip, the artist's sister-in-law, of the contents of Whistler's studio at his death.

The American painter had paid only one visit to Scotland in his youth, but there are a number of reasons why he and his family were particularly well disposed to Glasgow.

In April 1891 Glasgow Corporation became the first public body anywhere to buy a painting by Whistler, *Arrangement in Grey and Black No. 2: Portrait of Thomas Carlyle.* Public recognition thus came late to the artist, already in his mid 50s, who felt embittered by the lack of appreciation by the English artistic establishment. This purchase had been the result of a petition initiated by E.A. Walton, one of the Glasgow Boys, a group of progressive Scottish painters who greatly admired Whistler's work. Their valuation of Whistler as the outstanding artist working in Britain may well also have influenced the University of Glasgow's decision to confer on him the honorary degree of Doctor of Laws in April 1903, a few months before his death. The President of the Royal Scottish Academy, Sir James Guthrie, another of the Glasgow Boys, and the Professor of English Literature, Walter Raleigh, appear to have been his principal sponsors. Although unable to attend the ceremony through illness, Whistler was much touched by the compliment and in his letter of thanks reminded the University of his Scottish ancestry. His mother was descended from Daniel MacNeill, chief of his clan, who had emigrated with some 60 MacNeills from the Isle of Skye to North Carolina in 1746. Whistler was proud of this Jacobite connection, even being a member of the Order of the White Rose of Wynnstay, a Jacobite club.

Whistler had acquired another important Scottish link through his marriage in 1888. His wife, Beatrice, was the daughter of the Scottish sculptor, John Birnie Philip. Whistler was devoted to her, and to her younger sisters, Ethel and Rosalind. The latter (1873-1958), nicknamed 'The Major' by Whistler, was his ward, personal assistant and finally heiress and executrix. Her decision in 1935 to present what she considered a representative collection of paintings, pastels, drawings and prints on condition that none of them should ever leave the University, was influenced by her friendship with the Walton family, for E.A. Walton had established himself in London and was, in Whistler's last days, his neighbour in Chelsea.

In 1935 E.A. Walton's son John, the Professor of Botany, was responsible for the Fine Art Collections of the University. Rosalind may also have remembered a letter of Whistler's of

Thomas Carlyle, 1872-73, Glasgow Art Gallery and Museum

E.A. Walton, *Helen Walton* 1895.
This was inspired by Whistler's Portrait of Mrs Walter Sickert.

among Whistler enthusiasts from the late 1880s onwards; notable among the former, David Croal Thomson and Alexander Reid, and among the latter, John James Cowan and Sir William Burrell.

The gift in 1935 included nine full-length portraits, a *Nocturne*, a Chilean seascape and choice examples of Whistler's more intimate late portraits, figure subjects, shop fronts and seascapes numbering 41 paintings in all. The donation also embraced a very substantial collection of pastels, etchings, lithographs, etching plates and Whistler's collection of oriental ceramics as well as 59 drawings by Beatrice, Whistler's wife. To this was added some 70 etchings and lithographs which were part of a much larger gift by Dr James A. McCallum between 1939 and 1948.

In 1954 Miss Birnie Philip made a further gift of all the letters and papers from the estate (housed in the University Library) and at her death bequeathed the remainder of the paintings, drawings, watercolours and prints from the studio, among them some of outstanding quality which she had probably kept in 1935 for personal and sentimental reasons, together with the furniture and silver that Whistler had owned.

This collection has been subsequently augmented by the bequest in 1955 of Joseph Whistler Revillon (1886-1955), the artist's great nephew. This principally comprises Whistler family portraits, and an important group of early Parisian and London etchings, and two scrapbooks of letters (University Library).

Since 1958 the University has, with limited funds, added two early paintings, the finest piece of furniture that Whistler decorated, *Harmony in Yellow and Gold: The Butterfly Cabinet*, over 60 etchings not previously in the collection, and a group of paintings, prints and drawings by Whistler's friends and followers.

Overall the Hunterian Art Gallery's collection includes 80 oil paintings, over 100 pastels, 16 sketchbooks, over 120 drawings and watercolours, over 390 etchings, over 150 lithographs, two mezzotints, 280 etching plates and eight lithographic stones.

1895 in her possession addressed to The Fine Art Society reading 'I will let things of mine go to Scotland or Ireland or America – I want no pictures or drawings in England'. Scottish art dealers and collectors too had been prominent

Head of a Peasant Woman c. 1855-5

Whistler was born in Lowell, Massachusetts, the son of a successful railway engineer, Major George Washington Whistler, who was invited to Russia by the Czar in 1842 to build the Moscow to St. Petersburg railway. There at the Imperial Academy of Science Whistler received his first artistic training. On his father's premature death the family returned to America in 1849. After a false start as a cadet at the United States Military Academy, West Point from 1851 to 1854, and a brief period with the U.S. Coast and Geodetic Survey where he learnt the rudiments of etching, he embarked on his artistic career proper in Paris in 1855. He attended the Académie of the Swiss painter, Charles Gleyre and met a group of British art students including George Du Maurier and the future President of the Royal Academy, Edward Poynter. His sympathy, however, was more for contemporary French art. With two young French painters, Henri Fantin-Latour and Alphonse Legros he admired the work of Gustave Courbet, who rejected the current academic canons of art for a loudly-proclaimed realism. Whistler's few surviving early paintings, for instance the *Head of a Peasant Woman*, show a debt to Courbet in their subject matter, but owe more to Fantin-Latour and 17th century Dutch interior painters for low tones and careful lighting. A more lasting influence from Courbet was Whistler's realisation of the importance of self-advertisement. His early etchings, 'The French Set', were the result of a Rhineland sketching tour. These show his admiration for the prints of the Dutch 17th century masters, Rembrandt and Ruisdael, and for the work of the leading contemporary French etcher of the Barbizon School, Charles Jacque.

In 1859 Whistler moved to London, where his half-sister Deborah was living with her husband, the surgeon and amateur etcher, Seymour Haden. There he began 'The Thames Set' of etchings, notable for the meticulous depiction of dilapidated dockside warehouses. Unlike early topographical printmakers who drew the scene on paper and copied it on to the plate in the studio, Whistler drew direct on the plate in front of the subject – hence the greater spontaneity of appearance in Whistler's etchings.

Whistler's exhibits at the Royal Academy, *At the Piano* in 1860 and *The Coast of Brittany* in 1862, were well received, but reviewers of the later exhibitions of the decade remarked progressively more about his sketchiness, which contrasted strongly with the prevailing taste for high finish. The fluidity of his paint reveals an admiration for Velàzquez, whose work he studied in Manchester at the Art Treasures Exhibition in 1857 and in the Louvre. Aspects of the Spanish master's achievement inform many of his full-length portraits throughout his career.

Cartoon for Harmony in Blue and Gold: The Peacock Room 1876

In 1862 Whistler met Dante Gabriel Rossetti, the poet Algernon Swinburne, and others in the Pre-Raphaelite circle of artists. In the following year he became one of the first European artists to collect oriental arts and to introduce his own Japanese costumes, furniture, fans and ceramics into his compositions. Stimulated by contemporary interest in the interrelationships between the arts, Whistler started to adopt musical titles for his pictures, which he regarded as tone poems in paint. As his appreciation of Japanese prints grew, his compositions gained in subtlety and simplicity, as displayed in *Battersea Reach from Lindsey Houses* and *The Balcony*. In 1865 he struck up a close friendship with the painter Albert Moore, who shared his enthusiasm for the grace of Greek terracotta statuettes of the Hellenistic period from Tanagra. This interest is reflected in oils such as *Annabel Lee* and numerous pastels of nude or semi-nude adolescents that he continued to execute into the 1890s.

A group of seapieces of Valparaiso harbour that resulted from a brief trip to Chile in 1866 marked a break in style with the realistic description of his Thameside views. Twilight or night became his favourite setting in the *Nocturnes* of the 1870s, in which the warehouses and bridges were enveloped in low-keyed atmospheric hues. Following the teaching of the French theorist Lecoq de Boisbaudran, Whistler painted these in the studio from memory aided only by a few notes made on the spot – a practice that contrasted strongly with the *plein-air* painting of the Impressionists and his younger contemporary Bastien-Lepage and his followers. The title *Nocturne* with its musical overtones was suggested to Whistler by his patron, the Liverpool shipowner, F.R. Leyland. Leyland's London dining room was the site of Whistler's most ambitious decorative scheme, *The Peacock Room* of 1876-77, a cartoon for which is in the Hunterian Art Gallery. As the setting for one of his most elaborate orientalising portraits, this was richer and more exotic than his other interior designs. In general he strove for an elegance and delicacy through simple bands of light colour, which contrasted strongly with contemporary Victorian design. It was Whistler's *Nocturnes* that the influential critic John Ruskin deplored, leading to the famous libel suit of 1878. The farthing damages he won may have been a pyrrhic victory leading to the artist's bankruptcy, but by his art and his polemical pamphlets in the 1870s and 1880s he encouraged the more progressive artists and collectors to turn away from the literal and anecdotal approach dominant among exhibitors at the Royal Academy – the painters of 'the

Battersea Reach from Lindsey Houses c. 1864-71

Colour Scheme for the Dining Room, Aubrey House c. 1873

The broken line employed in the etchings is also found in his jewel-like Venetian pastels, more vibrant with colour than any other of his works.

From his return from Venice onwards much of Whistler's work became more intimate. Turning his back on the Thames he painted oils and watercolours of the shop fronts in Chelsea and the City. Many of his etchings and lithographs were vignettes; he explained his method to his pupil Mortimer Menpes. 'I begin first of all by seizing upon the chief point of interest. Perhaps it might have been the extreme distance – the little palaces and the shipping beneath the bridge. If so, I would begin drawing the distance in elaborately, and then would expand from it, until I come to the bridge which I would draw in the one broad sweep. If by chance I did not see the whole of the bridge, I would not put it in.' In Brittany, on the northern French Coast and in Holland he painted a series of exquisite small-scale seascapes, perhaps the freshest and most immediate of all his paintings. Many of his portraits were now devoted to children or family, and are particularly well represented in this collection. One or two little interiors painted in Paris in the 1890s such as *Miss Ethel Philip Reading* are akin to the contemporary work of the *Intimistes,* Bonnard and Vuillard. Not all his late work, however, was small scale. He was never short of commissions for full-length portraits to which much of his time was devoted. Growing evermore a perfectionist he was constantly rubbing down and altering these pictures in order to achieve the desired balance of line and colour. Hence the many unfinished canvases. Nevertheless these *Harmonies* and *Arrangements* include several brilliant successes, such as *Rose et Argent: La Jolie Mutine*, displaying an apparently effortless breadth and precisely calculated tonality compared with the tighter works of the 1870s.

British subject' he repeatedly derided. Whistler became 'The Master' for a growing group of followers and was eventually to be the most influential painter working in Britain in the last 20 years of the 19th century.

Financed by The Fine Art Society Whistler set off for Venice in 1879 to repair his fortunes. There he produced some of his most elaborate and celebrated etchings. In these he relied on an infinite variation of tone and texture in each plate to create poetic visions of the island city.

Chinese early 19th century Goldfish Bowl

Dutch 18th century Milk Jug

Whistler lived in uncluttered surroundings that matched the restrained tonality of his paintings. His furniture, some of which is on display, included a French empire style suite painted in pale blue, a late 18th century Bergère chair and some plain late 19th century English armchairs. On his marriage to Beatrice Godwin he avidly sought out English, Dutch and Irish silver of the Georgian period at silversmiths and jewellers in London and Paris. Each piece was engraved with the butterfly monograph he designed by the London firm Robert Dicker to indicate his ownership. His taste in silver was admired by visitors to his dining table, and The Fine Art Society in 1902 exhibited some of the choicest pieces.

The collection of oriental blue and white ceramics now in the Hunterian Art Gallery amounts to over 300 pieces dating from the late 17th to the 19th century. Whistler, a great admirer of Oriental art, had been one the earliest collectors in Britain of 'blue and white'. From the early 1860s he had amassed his first collection which was sold following his bankruptcy in 1879. Acquired when prices were low and competition slight, that collection was undoubtedly higher in quality than the pieces that Whistler could purchase in the late 1880s and 1890s. Whistler prized his 'blue and white', occasionally incorporating it in his paintings and using it frequently for entertaining. His biographers, the Pennells, record a lavish breakfast in Paris in 1893 with 'the good wine from the Abbé's cellar, the Argenteuil asparagus, the strawberries in a little silver basket at each guest's plate as well as "the beautiful blue and white." '

Brown and Gold 1895-1900

and critics, Baudelaire and Gautier, he attacked the contemporary wisdom that demanded the imitation of nature. He proclaimed that 'Nature contains the elements in colour and form, of all pictures, as the keyboard contains the notes of all music. But the artist is born to pick and choose, and group with science these elements, that the result may be beautiful – as the musician gathers his notes, and forms his chords, until he brings forth from chaos glorious harmony'.

When asked at the 1878 Ruskin libel trial for a definition of a *Nocturne* Whistler replied, 'I have perhaps meant rather to indicate an artistic interest alone in the work, divesting the picture from any outside anecdotal interest, which might have been otherwise attached to it'. So it was natural that Whistler held that the artist had the right to choose his subject from the contemporary world rather than derive it from the past. Hence for him the Thameside chimneys in the evening mist became 'Campanili – and the warehouses, palaces in the night' just as 'Rembrandt saw picturesque grandeur and noble dignity in the Jews' quarter of Amsterdam'.

The subject matter and execution of many of his riverscapes and townscapes offended against the canons of contemporary academic taste, lacking the grandeur of material or recognisable references to the art of the past and the elaboration of detail and high finish demanded by convention. Whistler's lecture, republished with other artistic statements in *The Gentle Art of Making Enemies* in 1892, reinforced the position already established in his art. The influence of his theory was to be widespread among following generations of artists. For instance Whistler's statement that a Nocturne 'is an arrangement of line, form and colour first' is echoed in Maurice Denis' celebrated dictum of 1890 that 'a picture before being a war-horse, a nude woman or some sort of anecdote – is essentially a surface covered with colours arranged in a certain order'.

For the public in the last quarter of the 19th century Whistler had a greater reputation as a controversial pamphleteer and acerbic wit than as a painter. In fact his pugnacious writings tended to impede contemporary appreciation of his art, outside a relatively limited circle of critics and patrons. Nevertheless in the long run his views on art were as influential as his art itself. They were principally expressed in the famous *Ten O'Clock Lecture*, first delivered at the Prince's Hall, London in 1885.

Following the precedent of the French poets

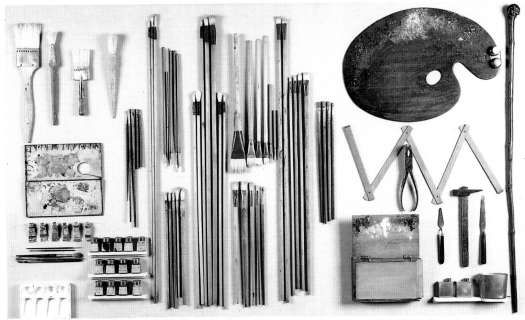

A selection of Whistler's painting equipment

Included in Miss Birnie Philip's gift were two trunks containing Whistler's painting equipment, together with one of his studio easels. Whistler was a stickler for making proper preparations before embarking on a painting. 'I do not teach art. I teach the scientific application of paint and brushes.' He recommended a small oval palette as being easy to handle and stressed the importance of harmony in the palette. 'White was placed at the top edge in the centre in generous quantity, and to the left came yellow, raw Sienna, raw umber, cobalt and mineral blue, while to the right vermilion, Venetian red, Indian red and black.' He was famous for his use of very long brushes, the hogs hair bristles bound with twine to straight dowels, which were made specially for him. With these he could work at a good distance, the better to observe the relationship between his subject and his canvas while painting full-length portraits.

However, he also used virtually every other type of brush that the invention of the metal ferrule for holding and shaping the brush head had made available to artists during his lifetime. A selection are on permanent display. Dating probably from late in Whistler's career, they are virtually identical to brushes produced today. Other equipment exhibited includes varnishing and priming brushes, palette knives and one of several small oil-sketching boxes containing primed panels, held in slides to prevent spoiling the completed work. The oil paints are still workable in their collapsible lead tubes, while the bottles of ground dry pigment were probably used for watercolour and gouache work.

There is also an extensive collection of Whistler's printmaking tools, and some of these, together with etching plates and a lithographic stone of his, have been incorporated into a permanent display of printmaking techniques in the Print Gallery.

Albert Moore, *Sketch for Reading Aloud* 1881-84

The Hunterian collection contains paintings, drawings and prints by several artists associated with Whistler. Albert Moore's *Sketch for Reading Aloud,* an oil painted on glass, a study for a picture in Glasgow Art Gallery and Museum, shows Whistler's friend sharing similar interests in classical sculpture and colour harmonies. The naive painter and Chelsea boatman Walter Greaves was Whistler's devoted assistant and follower, who imitated Whistler's *Nocturnes* of the Thames and fireworks at Cremorne Gardens. Walter Sickert, Whistler's best known pupil, painted his tiny seascape *Clodgy Point* alongside 'The Master' at St. Ives, Cornwall, whilst small paintings by the Australian Mortimer Menpes demonstrate his immense debt to Whistler. More individual was the approach of painters like Sidney Starr, who were admirers rather than pupils, as may be seen in his atmospheric *Figures on the Seashore.* The enthusiasm of the more progressive Scottish artists, particularly the Glasgow Boys, for Whistler's work is clearly seen in George Henry's *River Landscape by Moonlight* and John Lavery's *Contemplation* and even J.D.

Fergusson, 40 years younger than Whistler, later to be one of the Scottish Colourists, showed his admiration in his early *El Grao, Valencia.*

Sidney Starr, *Figures on the Seashore*

PLATES

Black Lion Wharf   1859

Etching. 14.9 x 22.4 cm. Third state of three.
Presented by Dr James A. McCallum.

Among Whistler's earliest works on leaving Paris for London in May 1859 were a group of eight etchings of the buildings on the banks of the Thames just below the Tower of London, the wharves between St. Katharine's Docks and Limehouse. Over eight weeks from August until October Whistler drew 'tumble-down bankside buildings – where all is pitchy and tarry, and corny and coally, and ancient and fishlike' staying for part of the time in an inn on the south bank in Rotherhithe. He may have been alerted to the possibilities of the area by seeing John Roddam Spencer Stanhope's *Thoughts of the Past* on exhibition at the Royal Academy in May with its view of warehouses on the Thames near Blackfriars in the background. He also undoubtedly had in mind the recent etchings of vanishing Paris by Charles Meryon (1821-68).

Whistler drew the image of *Black Lion Wharf* in reverse on the plate, possibly refreshing his memory from a drawing or photograph, so that the buildings appear the right way round in the etching. He probably sat at the foot of Horselydown New Stairs, just to the west of St. Saviour Dock, looking directly across the river to Black Lion Wharf on the right, whilst at the left lay the Hermitage Basin entrance to London Docks and beyond that the huge warehouse of Hoare and Co's Red Lion Brewery. Most of this area has completely disappeared in the post-war redevelopment of London's dockland.

Whistler describes these warehouses with a detail that owes much to the example of Meryon, but also to the accuracy of the Bohemian emigré etcher, Wenceslaus Hollar (1607-77), whose realistic views of the City of London from the Thames were well known to Whistler from the collection of his brother-in-law, Seymour Haden (1818-1910).

The contemporary French writer and collector, Philippe Burty, recognised in Whistler's use of prominent foreground 'figures and objects which he interprets without modelling, and in a relatively exaggerated scale' an affinity to photography, of which there had been a major exhibition in Paris held by the *Société française de photographie* in 1859. An equally valid parallel are those paintings of John Everett Millais (1829-96) which Whistler had taken his friend Fantin-Latour to see at the Royal Academy on 11 July, shortly before he began work on his Thames etchings.

The etching was well received when finally published in 1871 by Ellis and Green, King Street, Covent Garden in an edition of 100 after steel facing. It was the first in the portfolio of *A Series of Sixteen Etchings of Scenes on the Thames and Other Subjects,* otherwise known as 'The Thames Set'. The critic of *The Athenaeum* wrote 'here cranes, wooden galleries of delicious picturesqueness, and rarity, bow-windows, an "orange clipper", with raking spars, being those of a three-master schooner, steps that the tide has set awry, a lofty and smoking chimney, and the like incidents, supply a perfect treasure of materials, of which Mr Whistler is the master.' *The Saturday Review* described it as 'a work decisive and precise in execution, emphatic where emphasis is needed, brilliant in contrast of dark and light, delicate in the handling of unobtrusive passages, slight and sketchy in the treatment of episode'.

15

The Morning after the Revolution: Valparaiso   1866

Oil on canvas.   76.0 x 63.5 cm.

Presented by Miss Rosalind Birnie Philip, 1935.

This is one of half a dozen pictures that Whistler painted during his mysterious visit to Chile in 1866. Whistler himself told his biographers that he had gone to South America to help the Chileans and Peruvians fight against the Spanish. He may have felt embarassed as a former cadet at the West Point Military Academy not to have taken part in the American Civil War on the Southern side alongside his brother, Dr William Whistler. Recently it has been suggested that he fled Britain because of his friendship with the Irish patriot, John O'Leary (1830-1907), joint-editor of the republican newspaper, *Irish People*. O'Leary was sentenced to 20 years penal servitude for High Treason in December 1865 at a time when the threat of the Fenian revolutionary movement was received with hysteria by the English press. Whistler's correspondence with O'Leary was seized by the Dublin police.

On 2 February 1866, after making a will in favour of his mistress Jo Hiffernan and telling his close friend, the poet Swinburne, that he was going to California, he sailed for Panama from Southampton. He crossed the isthmus by land and boarded another steamer, which took him south via Peru to Valparaiso, where he arrived on 12 March putting up in the English Club at the invitation of a Mr McQueen. Just over a fortnight later, on the morning of 31 March, a Spanish naval squadron bombarded the city from the sea. It is to this event that the title of the picture refers. This title is inaccurate as there was no revolution, but Whistler may have invented it many years later when his memory of events had become dim. Chile and its ally, Peru, had obtained *de facto* independence from Spain much earlier in the century, but in 1863 a Spanish fleet arrived in the Pacific in an attempt to regain its former territories, seizing the Chincha Islands, valuable for their guano, in the following year. The Peruvians' ally, Chile, refused to salute the Spanish admiral and seized a Spanish schooner in November 1865, precipitating the attack on Valparaiso. The war continued in a desultory fashion until 1871.

Little evidence of the conflict appears in Whistler's picture. The harbour, seen from above, perhaps from a window of the English Club, with the quay forming a diagonal wedge at the left is compositionally reminiscent of the colour woodcuts of the Japanese artist, Hiroshige. That his work was well known to Whistler at this date – and probably represented in his collection of Japanese prints – is attested by the woodcuts visible in his painting of 1864 *Caprice in Purple and Gold: The Golden Screen* (Freer Gallery of Art, Washington D.C.). Virtually the same composition recurs in another Valparaiso picture *Nocturne in Blue and Gold: Valparaiso Bay* (Freer Gallery of Art, Washington D.C.). Whistler painted his first *Nocturnes* in Chile as well as twilight and dawn views of Valparaiso harbour.

The style and tonality of this picture and the liquidity of the paint has parallels in a series of pictures of American Civil War naval subjects by Whistler's friend, Edouard Manet (1832-1883), which Whistler may well have seen on exhibition in Paris in 1864 and 1865, *The Battle of the Kearsage and the Alabama* (Philadelphia Museum of Art), *The Kearsage at Boulogne* (Private Collection) and *The Steam Boat* (Art Institute of Chicago).

Sketch for 'The Balcony'   1867
Oil on wood. 61.0 x 48.2 cm.
Bequeathed by Miss Rosalind Birnie Philip, 1958.

The prominent grid marking, particularly notice-able in the bottom third of the picture, was made by Whistler in preparation for transferring the design of this painting onto a larger support, a method of enlarging commonly used by artists. In this case there is no evidence of the com-position ever being transferred. The picture is closely related to a watercolour in the Hunterian's collection, and another oil panel *Variations in Flesh Colour and Green: The Balcony* (Freer Gallery of Art, Washington D.C.), which was begun in 1864 and exhibited at the Royal Academy in 1870 (468). In about January 1867 Whistler wrote to Fantin-Latour that he was planning to enlarge to lifesize *'La petite esquisse du balcon'* for the Paris Salon. According to his friend George Boughton who saw it in the 1870s, Whistler regarded the Freer picture as 'too much elaborated, not nearly simple enough'. Both the Freer picture and the watercolour are almost identical in size to the sketch. The composition of the former was probably transferred via the watercolour, which is on tracing paper, to this panel.

The figures in the sketch were originally very close to those of both the other versions and subsequently adjusted, most noticeably the head of the girl second from the right was lowered and the arm of the standing figure moved to grasp the balcony. More dramatic was the change in colour from a rather cold tonality with the icy grey Thames and factory chimneys in the background to a more generalised composition with a much warmer and more harmonious colour scheme and a more limited range of colours, closer to that of a series of paintings known as 'The Six Projects' (Freer Gallery of Art, Washington D.C.).

Whistler's American apprentice, Clifford Addams relates that Whistler acquired a set of little Japanese dolls, which he used in arranging the figures in this composition. A Japanese doll is seen in a photograph of one of the rooms in his house, taken shortly after his death. The essence of the composition probably derives from a woodcut by Torii Kiyonaga in Whistler's collection (British Museum, London) *The Fourth Month* from his series *Twelve Months in the South* of 1784, while the pose of the seated girl second from the right appears to be drawn from another Kiyonaga woodcut *Autumn Moon on the Sumida*.

Sketch for 'Annabel Lee' *c.* 1869
Oil on wood. 30.7 x 22.6 cm.
Bequeathed by Miss Rosalind Birnie Philip, 1958.

The Glasgow Liberal M.P. William Graham
(1817-85) commissioned a painting of Annabel
Lee from Whistler in 1869, which was never
delivered as the artist never considered that he had
completed it to his satisfaction. Eventually in
1877 Whistler asked his patron to accept another
painting, *Nocturne: Blue and Gold: Old
Battersea Bridge* (Tate Gallery) for the £100 that
he had advanced. The unfinished painting,
Annabel Lee, originally intended for Graham,
survives in a rubbed down state in the Hunterian
Art Gallery. It has been suggested that this sketch
is a recapitulation of the subject, but its handling
and tonality is comparable to the *Sketch for 'The
Balcony'* (p. 19).

Graham was an important collector of Italian
paintings of the period before 1500, and a patron
of Edward Burne-Jones (1833-98) and Dante
Gabriel Rossetti (1828-82). This may explain the
theme from literature, a great rarity in Whistler's
work. The painter abhorred the story-telling detail
of the subject pictures which occupied so much
space and received so much critical attention at
the exhibitions of the Royal Academy and other
institutions during the mid Victorian period.

The title of the painting is that of the poem by
Whistler's compatriot, Edgar Allan Poe – like
Whistler a former cadet of the West Point Military
Academy – whose work he much admired. The
poem, which is printed here, may well have
appealed precisely because it gave no information
about Annabel Lee, except that she lived by the
sea. The painting is one of many variations on a
theme that obsessed Whistler in drawings and
paintings, that of diaphanously clad girls lounging
on a balcony against a backdrop of sea and sky.

ANNABEL LEE.

It was many and many a year ago,
    In a kingdom by the sea,
That a maiden there lived whom you may know
    By the name of ANNABEL LEE;
And this maiden she lived with no other thought
    Than to love and be loved by me.

I was a child and *she* was a child,
    In this kingdom by the sea:
But we loved with a love that was more than love…
    I and my ANNABEL LEE;
With a love that the winged seraphs of heaven
    Coveted her and me.

And this was the reason that, long ago,
    In this kingdom by the sea,
A wind blew out of a cloud, chilling
    My beautiful ANNABEL LEE;
So that her highborn kinsman came
    And bore her away from me,
To shut her up in a sepulchre
    In this kingdom by the sea.

The angels, not half so happy in heaven,
    Went envying her and me…
Yes!…that was the reason (as all men know,
    In this kingdom by the sea)
That the wind came out of the cloud by night,
    Chilling and killing my ANNABEL LEE.

Florence Leyland Seated *c.* 1870

Chalk. 28.3 x 18.4 cm. Signed with a butterfly.
Presented by Miss Rosalind Birnie Philip, 1935

Whistler's most important patron from the mid 1860s until the mid 1870s was the Liverpool shipowner, Frederick R. Leyland (1831-1892), to whom he had been introduced by Dante Gabriel Rossetti. Initially Leyland purchased *La Princesse du Pays de la Porcelaine* (Freer Gallery of Art, Washington D.C.) and then commissioned *The Three Girls* (destroyed) and a series of portraits of himself, his wife and his children. It was Leyland who suggested the title *Nocturne* for Whistler's moonlights. Between 1869 and 1875 Whistler was a regular visitor to Speke Hall, Leyland's Tudor manor house, near Liverpool, where he worked on the portraits, falling in love with Mrs Leyland's younger sister, Elizabeth Dawson, to whom he was briefly engaged. However, a bitter quarrel broke out over the payment for the decoration of Leyland's dining room at Princes Gate, London, *The Peacock Room,* which Whistler undertook in 1876 to provide a suitable setting for *La Princesse du Pays de la Porcelaine.* This resulted in their complete estrangement.

This drawing is one of six portraits in the Hunterian's collection of Florence (born 1859), second of the three Leyland daughters, who married the painter Val Prinsep (1836-1904) in 1884. Whistler also painted a full-length oil of her in 1876 (Portland Art Museum) for which he made a number of costume studies, and executed an etching of her holding a hoop in 1873. Some of his drawings of the Leyland children may have been exhibited at his first one-man exhibition at the Flemish Gallery, 48 Pall Mall in 1874. Some were acquired by Mrs Florence Leyland, Frederick's wife, but none by Leyland himself. The critic of *The Academy,* Sidney Colvin praised his portraits of young girls as 'altogether exquisite' and as showing 'a charm as well as a vividness and address which to my mind put them at the head of all Mr Whistler's engraved work. The same qualities occur in a brilliant degree in some of the studies on the lowest tier.'

In this drawing Whistler used vigorous strokes of the chalk to create the ruffles and shimmer of the little girl's dress, whilst a much more sensitive and delicate touch captures her flowing hair and tense look. The butterfly signature is carefully placed to form part of the design. Whistler developed this form of signature from his initials JMW in the late 1860s, in imitation of the seal signatures on Japanese prints. His butterflies subsequently became less stiff and formal evolving into freer and more calligraphic shapes. Some indeed turned into mocking self-portraits.

Blue and Silver: Screen with Old Battersea Bridge 1871-1872

Distemper and gold paint on brown paper laid on canvas framed in two hinged panels.
195.0 x 182.0 cm. Signed with a butterfly on the frame.
Bequeathed by Miss Rosalind Birnie Philip, 1958.

The impetus for this work arose from Whistler's acquisition of two Japanese screen panels, which he reused to create a composition of his own on the reverse. The paintings, in watercolour and bodycolour on silk, are by a contemporary artist, Osawa Nampo (b. 1845), working at the Meirindo-studio, Tokyo, signed and dated July and August 1867. The peach tree and blossoms do not form a continuous design, which suggests the panels come from a larger, perhaps four-fold, screen, or are even parts from two screens. The frame is not Japanese, and is probably to Whistler's design, and he decorated the gilded wood on both sides with a four and five petal flower pattern in two shades of green in harmony with the colour of his painting.

Whistler's painting was at one time intended for Frederick Leyland and exhibited with his portraits of Mr and Mrs Leyland at his one-man show in 1874. It must have been deposited with a friend or dealer to prevent its inclusion in Whistler's bankruptcy sale. Although he later entrusted the screen to the dealer C.W. Dowdeswell and in 1892 exhibited it at Goupil's smaller gallery in London, he was clearly greatly attached to it and took it with him to his Paris studio in the rue Notre Dame des Champs.

The painting shows the Thames at night from the south bank with the clocktower of Chelsea Church on the left, a pier of Old Battersea Bridge, and in the far distance the Albert Bridge. Whistler made several preliminary chalk and pastel drawings, now in the Hunterian Art Gallery, the Freer Gallery of Art, Washington D.C., and the Albright-Knox Art Gallery, Buffalo. The drawing in Buffalo appears to have been an experiment to test the effect of folding, as it has a vertical crease at the point in the painting where the screen was to be hinged.

Whistler's earliest picture of Old Battersea Bridge of 1859 (Addison Gallery of American Art, Andover, Massachusetts) is thickly painted and filled with detail. In this Screen and the contemporaneous *Nocturne: Blue and Gold – Old Battersea Bridge* (Tate Gallery, London), he pays open homage to the masters of the Japanese print in the simplification of the composition, low viewpoint, emphasis on the vertical piles of the bridge and prominent moon. No exact source can be isolated, but the pictures bear resemblances in composition to Hiroshige's *Kyo Bridge* and Hokusai's *Mannenbashi Bridge*.

This is Whistler's only surviving distemper painting though he probably used the medium for his wall decorations at Aubrey House and Lindsey Row. He used the same verdigris blue obtained from Freemans, Battersea for his *Harmony in Blue and Gold: The Peacock Room* decorated in 1876 for Frederick Leyland.

Harmony in Yellow and Gold: The Butterfly Cabinet 1877-78

Mahogany with ceramic tiling, glass and brass edgings decorated in part with gold leaf and oil paint. 303.0 x 190.0 x 46.0 cm. Signed with a butterfly.
Purchased with the aid of the National Art-Collections Fund, 1973.

In the autumn of 1877 the architect Edward William Godwin (1833-86), a close friend of Whistler and fellow enthusiast for Japanese art, was asked to design a fireplace with shelves as an exhibition stand for the London furnishing manufacturer, William Watt. A preliminary drawing for it is dated 22 September 1877 (Victoria and Albert Museum). In the winter of 1877-78 Godwin suggested that Whistler should paint a surrounding dado. Whistler eventually decorated the panels at the back of all the shelves as well with Japanese clouds, chrysanthemum petals and butterflies, using gilding to highlight areas that might otherwise have been in deep shadow. Whistler had to repaint it in March 1878 'due to the blundering of Mr Watt's men' before its despatch to the Paris 1878 *Exposition Universelle*. Whistler's decoration extended above the dado to the yellow wallpaper surrounding the fireplace which he signed with a butterfly.

In Paris it housed a display of oriental porcelain lent by Liberty's. A photograph of part of the stand shows a spindly occasional table and a small chair with Japanese fretwork on its back designed by Godwin, much more oriental in style than the cabinet. That *The Butterfly Cabinet* is much more ponderous than most of Godwin's furniture may be due to its purpose.

The correspondent of the *New York Daily Tribune* noted that the 'Kaga porcelain on the shelves' was 'chosen for the yellowness of the red, which is a characteristic of that ware' and went on to describe the complete setting 'on a yellowish-brown velvet rug. Chairs and sofas were covered with yellow, pure rich yellow velvet, darker in shade than the yellow of the wall, and edged with a yellow fringe. The framework of the sofa has a hint of the Japanese influence which faintly, but only faintly, suggests itself through the room. Its lattice-work back and wheel-patterned ends might pass for bamboo, the carpentry is as light as if the long fingers of a saffron-faced artist had coaxed it into shape'. The reviewer noted the incongruence of William Watt's sign which 'stares you in the face at the top in a way which would drive Mr Whistler mad if he saw it, for in his fancies below, there is no suggestion of the shop.'

The Building News praised the design for 'a charming simplicity', its elegance in its mouldings and its freedom 'from the artificial and operose look common in much of modern furniture'. *The Magazine of Art* preferred to call it an 'agony in yellow'.

Subsequently the Butterfly Cabinet was incorporated into the White House, Chelsea, which Godwin had designed for Whistler, but on 18 September 1879 the house and its contents were sold following Whistler's bankruptcy. Some years later the collector Pickford Waller (1849-1930) discovered the piece in a second-hand furniture shop and having no use for it as a fireplace converted it into a cabinet by replacing the grate with doors adapted from the dado panels. It was on his daughter's death in 1973 that it was sold at auction and acquired by the Hunterian Art Gallery. The oriental ceramics displayed on the upper shelves are drawn from Whistler's own collection.

Nocturne 1879-80
Etching and drypoint. 20.0 x 29.5 cm. Fourth state of four.
Signed in pencil with a butterfly on tab.
Purchased (McCallum Fund), 1965.

Whistler originally planned a visit to Venice during the summer of 1876 when 14 subscribers promised £693 for sets of 12 Venice etchings at 50 guineas each. The trip was eventually made possible by The Fine Art Society after Whistler's bankruptcy in May 1879. This newly-established firm offered him a chance to regain financial security by advancing him £150 to enable him to spend three months in Venice to make the set, whilst retaining the option of buying the plates for £700 on his return. He left London early in September, intending to return in December, but in the event stayed until November 1880 producing no less than 50 etchings.

This view was taken from the Riva degli Schiavoni, close to the Casa Jankovitz, where Whistler later stayed with a group of young American painters and printmakers known as 'the Duveneck Boys' after Frank Duveneck (1848-1919), their master. The church and campanile of San Giorgio Maggiore can be seen on the right and the dome of Santa Maria della Salute on the left. This is in reverse to nature, for Whistler, drawing directly on the plate, did not normally trouble to counter the reversing effect of printing. Whistler began work in 1879 on the plate, which was published in 'The First Venice Set' in 1880, and exhibited at The Fine Art Society late that November. *Nocturne* was singled out by the reviewer in *British Architect* as 'different in treatment to the rest of the prints, and (it) can hardly be called, as it stands an etching; the bones as it were of the picture have been etched, which bones consist of some shipping and distant objects, and then over the whole of the plate ink has apparently been smeared.' The writer was perceptive in recognising the radical nature of the print. Indeed individual impressions vary widely in appearance depending on Whistler's mani-pulation of ink on the plates. By wiping the ink with his hand or with muslin he created differing effects of luminosity, atmosphere and time of day. In this case Whistler's very sparing use of line combined with his carefully calculated layer of plate tone creates a magical effect of ships and churches emerging indistinctly out of the gathering dusk.

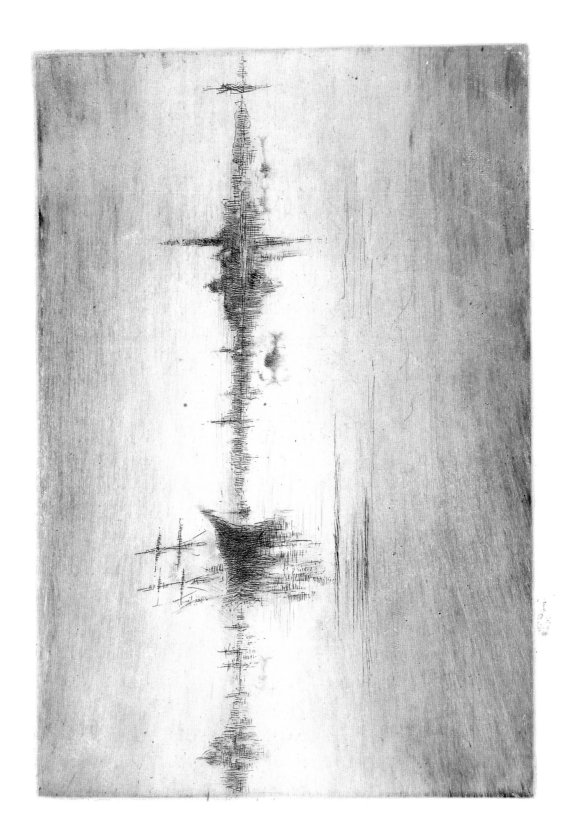

Salute: Sundown   1880
Pastel. 20.0 x 26.8 cm. Signed with a butterfly.
Bequeathed by Miss Rosalind Birnie Philip, 1958.

Whistler was unable to do much etching on his arrival in Venice in 1879 due to the inclement weather. In answer to an angry letter from Marcus Huish of The Fine Art Society complaining about the delay over receiving his plates he wrote in January 1880: 'I can't fight against the Gods – with whom I am generally a favourite – and not come to grief – so that now – at this very moment – I am an invalid and a prisoner – because I rashly thought I might hasten matters by standing in the snow with a plate in my hand and an icicle at the end of my nose. – I was ridiculous – the Gods saw it and sent me to my room in disgrace.... Here in Venice there has been a steady hardening of every faculty belonging to the painter for the last two months and a half at least – during which time you might as well have proposed to etch on a block of Wenham Lake as to have done anything with a copper plate that involves holding it.' So he turned to pastels instead. Whistler was presumably alluding to the lake at Little Wenham, south-west of Ipswich in Suffolk, which freezes in severe winters.

This is one of a number of views of the Baroque church of Santa Maria della Salute on the Grand Canal, the masterpiece of the Venetian architect, Baldassare Longhena (1598-1682). It was probably drawn from the quay in front of the Piazzetta, repeating a view that he had already captured in one of his earliest etchings in Venice, *Nocturne: Salute*. Though apparently effortless the large number of pinholes at the top corners indicate the pains which Whistler took in different sessions to achieve satisfactory results.

According to his compatriot and fellow lodger Bacher, 'In beginning a pastel he drew his subject crisply and carefully in outline with black crayon upon one of these sheets of tinted paper which fitted the general color of the motive. A few touches with sky-tinted pastels, corresponding to nature, produced a remarkable effect, with touches of red, grays and yellows for the buildings here and there!' He carried with him everywhere 'two boxes of pastels, an older one for instant use, filled with little bits of strange, broken colors of which he was very fond, a newer box with which

he did his principal work. He had quantities of vari-coloured papers, browns, reds, greys, uniform in size.'

In all Whistler made over 100 pastels, 53 of which he exhibited on his return at The Fine Art Society in January 1881, the most successful of all his exhibitions in his lifetime. The gallery was decorated according to Whistler's instruction. His mistress, Maud Franklin described it as 'an arrangement in brown and gold and Benedictine red which is very lovely!' E.W. Godwin, the architect and designer described it more fully: 'First, a low skirting of yellow-gold, then a high dado of dull yellow-green cloth, then a moulding of green-gold, and then a frieze and ceiling of pale reddish brown. The frames are arranged on the line, but here and there one is placed over another. Most of the frames and mounts are a rich yellow gold, but a dozen out of the fifty three are in green gold dotted about with a view to decoration, and eminently successful in attaining it!'

Godwin singled out *Salute: Sundown* as one of the 'masterpieces' in the show 'not merely in the use of pastel, but in the use of the tinted paper..., in the choice of subject and in its treatment.'

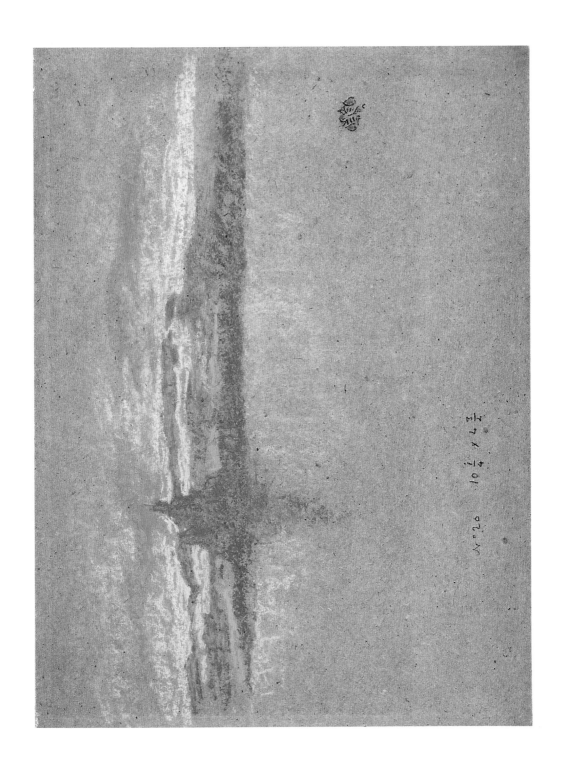

Terry's Fruit Shop, Chelsea   *c.* 1887
Watercolour. 12.6 x 20.5 cm. Signed with a butterfly.
Presented by Miss Rosalind Birnie Philip, 1935.

This shop at 45 Cheyne Walk was one of
Whistler's local fruit shops where he lived in
Chelsea for the last 20 years of his life. It was
owned by George Terrey, fruiterer and
greengrocer from 1881 until 1930. The spelling of
the title is that of Miss Philip.

In the 1880s Whistler executed a whole series
of small oil paintings, watercolours, lithographs
and etchings of shops, principally within walking
distance of his homes, but also elsewhere in
London and Paris. Mortimer Menpes recalled his
London pictures: 'Whistler would get his little
pochade box, and together we would drift out into
the open, – on to the Embankment, or down a side
street in Chelsea, – and he would make a little
sketch, sometimes in water, sometimes in oil
colour. It might be a fish shop with eels for sale at
so much a plate, and a few soiled children in the
foreground, or perhaps a sweet-stuff shop, and the
children standing with their faces glued to the
pane. There he would stay and paint until
luncheon time, sitting on rush-bottomed chairs
borrowed from the nearest shop.'

Menpes justly remarked that in contrast to his
low-toned oils 'his watercolours were very fair
and delicate' and that he allowed the white paper
of his support as an extra colour.

The lady at the left is dressed in Bohemian
artistic costume which contrasts strongly with that
of the fashionably dressed lady at the right.

The Embroidered Curtain 1889
Etching and drypoint. 23.7 x 15.9 cm. Fifth state of seven.
Signed with a butterfly on tab.
Presented by Miss Rosalind Birnie Philip, 1935.

In 1889 Whistler was invited by the painter and writer, Philippe Zilcken (1857-1930), to show his work at the third exhibition of the Etching Club at The Hague. This invitation may have been one of the spurs to his visit in August 1889 to Amsterdam where he stayed at Brack's Doelen Hotel. He intended to make a set of ten etchings, hoping to sell the plates to The Fine Art Society for 2,000 guineas and to print editions of 30 impressions, each to be priced no less than ten guineas. He regarded the results as 'far finer work than anything I have hitherto produced' and spoke of the division of his etched work into three periods. 'First you see me at work on the Thames.... Now there you see the crude and hard detail of the beginner. So far, so good. There, you see, all is sacrificed to exactitude of outline. Presently, and almost unconsciously, I begin to criticise myself, and to feel the craving of the artist for form and colour. The result was the second stage, which my enemies call incohate, and I call Impressionism' (The Venice etchings). 'The third stage I have shown you. In that I have endeavored to combine stages one and two. You have the elaboration of the first stage and quality of the second.' 'The subjects' appealed to him 'most sympathetically'. For as he had stated of Rembrandt in *The Ten O'Clock Lecture* in 1885 he saw 'picturesque grandeur and noble dignity in the Jews' quarter of Amsterdam, and lamented not that its inhabitants were not Greeks'.

The Embroidered Curtain, also known as *The Lace Curtain,* is one of the 14 plates he executed in Amsterdam and its environs, but they were never issued as a set as the dealers found the price too high. The ornate late 17th century building represented, nos 52 and 54 Palmgracht in the Jordaan district, no longer exists. *The Pall Mall Gazette* praised the way 'the delicate tracery of the pattern' of the lace curtain 'has been worked out to the minutest detail'. In possibly the most intricately worked of all Whistler's etchings, the myriad of lines scattered like hairs over the plate create a shimmering effect of reflections in the window panes and the canal. In complete contrast to many of his earlier etchings there is no single area of interest isolated in a vignette. Yet despite the frontal presentation and the grid pattern of doors and windows which was picked up in the 'dainty frames of white with black bars' noted by a reviewer in which the Amsterdam prints were originally framed, Whistler still captures the majesty of the substantial merchants' houses.

WATER
en
VUUR

Red and Black: The Fan *c.*1891-94
Oil on canvas. 187.4 x 89.8 cm. Signed with a butterfly.
Bequeathed by Miss Rosalind Birnie Philip, 1958

This is the finest of six full-length portraits painted
by Whistler of his sister-in-law, Ethel Philip
(1861-1920), a favourite sitter in the late 1880s
and early 1890s. Whistler was particularly fond of
Ethel, Beatrice Whistler's younger sister. The
fourth daughter of John Birnie Philip, she acted as
Whistler's secretary in 1893-94 before her
marriage in 1894 to a man of letters, Charles
Whibley (1859-1930). Whibley was a correspondent of the *Scots Observer* (later *The National
Observer)*. Subsequently he became Paris
correspondent of the *Pall Mall Gazette* and for 30
years a contributor to *Blackwood's Magazine.*
Whistler, who referred to him as 'Wobbles',
designed the cover of his volume of essays, *A
Book of Scoundrels, 1897.*

 Whistler affectionately nicknamed Ethel
'Bunnie'. He was, according to the Pennells,
working at three full-length portraits of her at 110,
rue du Bac in 1894: this picture, *Mother of Pearl
and Silver: The Andalusian* (National Gallery of
Art, Washington) and *Rose et Or: La Tulipe*
(Hunterian Art Gallery). The Cleveland
industrialist, Alfred Atmore Pope, who owned five
Whistler oils, was anxious to have first refusal of
Red and Black: The Fan in November 1894. The
celebrated Boston collector, Isabella Stewart
Gardner, saw it in Paris and wanted to buy ' "the
red Bunnie!" not only because of all the
associations'. She obviously enjoyed meeting
Whistler and his sitter, as well as admiring the
canvas. However, Whistler told her that it was
already sold. This was obviously not true and it
remained in his studio. Though signed, the picture
was described as unfinished when exhibited
shortly after Whistler's death at the Royal Society
of Portrait Painters in November 1903 (4). In her
review of this exhibition in the *Daily Chronicle*
Elizabeth Robins Pennell complained that the
subtle tonal harmony of Whistler's picture was
broken into by the red of the wall behind it. As a
result the picture was 'rehung on special draperies
of a neutral tint' more sympathetic to the delicate
colour.

Draped Figure Reclining   *c.* 1891-93
Colour lithograph. 17.0 x 25.5 cm. Only state.
Presented by Miss Rosalind Birnie Philip, 1935.

Whistler made only seven colour lithographs,
which are extremely rare since no proper editions
were ever printed. After an initial experiment in
London in *c.* 1890 with the encouragement of the
lithographic printers, Thomas Way and his son,
Whistler returned to colour lithography in Paris in
the autumn of 1891. The elder Way was himself
attempting to reproduce Whistler's pastels in
colour. Whistler's interest may have been sparked
by the revival in the medium amongst French
artists, particularly Pierre Bonnard (1867-1947)
and Henri Toulouse-Lautrec (1864-1901) who
made their first colour lithographs in 1889 and
1891 respectively. Whistler planned to publish a
group of prints, *Songs on Stone,* through William
Heinemann. He worked with the printers Henry
Belfond in the rue Gaillon mixing his own colours
and standing alongside the press checking each
individual proof for the colour balance.

A stone was used for each colour, in this case
six, grey, green, pink, yellow, blue and purple, in
addition to the keystone which printed black. For
each stone Whistler made a separate drawing on
specially prepared semi-transparent transfer
paper. The drawings were then transferred to the
stones. To ensure correct registration Whistler
made four marks in the centre of each side of the
composition.

Hetty Pettigrew (p. 41) was probably the
model for *Draped Figure Reclining*, sometimes
known as *Study in Colour No. 2*. Whistler was in
the habit of making drawings one side of the
English Channel and posting or carrying them
across to the other for the transfer of the compositions to the stones. This lithograph is the
most complex and successful of his colour prints
– the only one that approaches the tonal subtlety
of his pastels of young female models. Sadly the
closure of Belfond's shop in 1894 due to his
bankruptcy and Whistler's quarrel with the Ways
in 1896 appears to have put an end to Whistler's
experiments with colour lithography.

The Arabian *c.* 1892
Pastel. 18.1 x 27.8 cm. Signed twice with a butterfly.
Presented by Miss Rosalind Birnie Philip, 1935.

Harriet Selina Pettigrew (born 1867), known affectionately as Hetty, the model for this pastel, was the eldest of three daughters of William Pettigrew, a cork cutter of Portsea Island near Portsmouth. A local art-master seeing the children told their mother 'you have a small fortune in these lovely little girls!'

Taking his hint and a bundle of introductory letters to leading London artists, Hetty and her sisters Rose Amy (born 1872) and Lilian (born 1870) came up to town in the early 1880s. They soon became extremely popular as artists' models because of their beauty. According to her sister Rose, Hetty had 'soft straight hair, like a burnished chestnut, glorious skin and big hazel eyes'.

All three sisters posed for John Everett Millais' *An Idyll of 1745* (Lady Lever Art Gallery, Port Sunlight), which was exhibited at the Royal Academy in 1884. Subsequently they posed for many of the leading painters and sculptors of the day, including Lord Leighton, Sir Edward Poynter, William Holman Hunt, John Sargent, Edward Onslow Ford and John Tweed, as well as for artists in the immediate circle of Whistler, such as Walter Sickert, Philip Wilson Steer and Theodore Roussel. Whistler found Hetty 'a perfect match for him, he admired her, and was very amused by her cleverly cruel sayings, even when it was against himself.' When Whistler failed to pay her model's fees, 'she refused to pose again unless she had her money. We never, *never* posed under half a guinea a day, which was a big sum in those days of cheapness. "Oh! Hetty dear, that is much too much", Whistler said. Hetty looked at him with a little sneer and said, "I'm so sorry, I'd quite forgotten you were one of the seven and sixpenny men!"'

Whistler began using the sisters as models *c.* 1890. This is one of the most sumptuous of his studies of them, many of which are in the Hunterian Art Gallery's collection. The sinuous curves of Hetty's youthful body are set off to perfection by the coloured drapery scattered in profusion over the cane couch. The intense oranges, reds, pale blues and violets in this drawing rival the brilliant tints of Persian miniatures. Such exuberance in colour is rare in the work of Whistler.

Blue and Silver: Belle Isle   1893
Watercolour.   21.6 x 13.0 cm. Signed with a butterfly.
Presented by Miss Rosalind Birnie Philip, 1935.

Whistler and his wife toured Brittany in July and
August 1893 painting a group of seascapes in oil
and watercolour. Whistler's attention may have
been drawn to Belle Isle, south of the Quiberon
peninsula off the west coast of Brittany, by his
friend Claude Monet (1840-1926), who had
painted there in 1886, and exhibited *Coast of Belle
Isle, Bretagne* at the Society of British Artists
(212) at Whistler's invitation that winter. The
actress and amateur painter, Sarah Bernhardt
(1845-1923), another friend of Whistler, acquired
a property on the isle the year of Whistler's visit.
    One of two watercolours of beachscapes
executed at Belle Isle now in the Hunterian Art
Gallery, *Blue and Silver,* in its narrow upright
formal and sparse composition recalls Japanese
prints.

The Thames 1896
Lithotint. 26.5 x 18.7 cm. Second state of three.
Bequeathed by Miss Rosalind Birnie Philip, 1958.

Whistler was introduced to the technique of the lithotint by the printer Thomas Way (1861-1913). Charles Hullmandel (1789-1850) had patented the technique in 1841, but after his initial collaboration with James Duffield Harding (1799-1863), it had largely lain unused by artists for over 30 years. It enabled the artist to combine a wash with a chalk outline in emulation of watercolour. This wash was created by dissolving chalk or crayon in water or ammonia. After making a group of eight lithotints in 1878 Whistler did not execute another for 18 years, perhaps because the wash tended to clog on the stone after the initial impressions were taken, resulting in unsatisfactorily smudged results. The artist had to spend many hours beside the printer scraping and re-etching the stone to achieve the delicate quality that he required.

In 1896 he was confined to the Savoy Hotel where his wife Beatrice lay dying of cancer. From his hotel window he produced the finest of his lithotints, *The Thames,* a view south-east across the river. Reversed on the stone to the left is Hungerford Railway Bridge and in the centre the Shot Tower. According to Way, Whistler worked from an oil study of the scene, a procedure unparalleled in his work. Using a stone prepared with a half-tint on the surface, Whistler went to great pains to emulate the beautiful tonal balance of *Grey and Silver: The Thames* of *c.* 1872 (Hunterian Art Gallery), carrying the stone back and forth from his room to the workshop, conveniently just across the street from Way's workshop at 21 Wellington Street, off The Strand, in order to check the quality of the printing. Twice he scraped out the light areas and added new elements to the design, taking six proofs of the first state, ten of the second and twelve of the final state.

He recognized that this was one of his most significant prints. He wrote to his dealer, E.G. Kennedy that it was 'promising to be very beautiful and from your late lectures to me very startling as it will cost probably something like ten guineas a proof!' One of the most beautiful and silvery of his nocturnes, it won a gold medal at the Paris International Exposition of 1899. The print matches the poetic quality of the painting and its silvery grey tonality. In the words of *The Glasgow Herald* of 1 June 1915 it 'is a particularly expressive nocturne. The slow, dull tide of the river, the dark, veiled shapes of factory chimneys and warehouses on the further shore, the sky of drifting clouds, have the poetry inherent in Whistler's view of such a scene fraught to him with beauty that touched his soul and gave it peace.'

Green and Gold: A Shop in Calais   1896
Oil on wood. 24.5 x 13.0 cm. Signed with a butterfly.
Presented by Miss Rosalind Birnie Philip, 1935.

In September 1896 Whistler spent two weeks
painting around Dieppe and on the coast of the
Pas de Calais. On 16 September he wrote to his
sister-in-law, Rosalind Birnie Philip, 'I am getting
very miserable with my struggles against the
weather. It either pours or is cold – and I don't see
the use in worrying on here.... I began a little shop
here – but it was a queer hard day today & I have
done no good.' The following day he wrote, 'I
have hung on here notwithstanding my half
intention of going further on my wanderings in the
hope of finishing one small shop I had begun.'
Finally on 19 September he wrote, 'this afternoon
only did I discover, thanks to the waiter at the
hotel a wonderful little bit of the town that might
have been a fortune – but I fear too late now – an
old Spanish scrap – quite marvelous (sic) – It may
do by and bye – and I will keep it to myself!'
Despite his troubles with the rain and cold
Whistler managed to produce one of his finest
shop front oils, which he probably exhibited at the
Société Nationale des Beaux Arts in 1897 (1257)
as *Vert et Violet*. The violet was not painted but
rather achieved by leaving the grey areas of the
primed panel visible particularly in the windows.
The gold and green have such an effect upon the
nearby grey as to make it seem violet to the eye.
He also allowed tiny patches of grey to show
through the yellow-gold and green of the shop to
create the effect of the watery conditions in which
he was painting in Calais. Whistler's practice of
using this priming for his small panels was much
imitated by his followers, most notably Walter
Sickert and Mortimer Menpes after their winter
spent painting beside him at St. Ives in Cornwall
in 1883-1884.

Little Juniper Bud: Lizzie Willis 1896-97
Oil on canvas. 51.6 x 31.4 cm.
Bequeathed by Miss Rosalind Birnie Philip, 1958.

This is one of three portraits that Whistler painted
of the daughter of his housekeeper at 8 Fitzroy
Street, a studio that he took in March 1896. The
Willis family had a fondness for alcohol, to which
the title surely refers since juniper berries are an
essential ingredient in flavouring gin. Whistler
described Lizzie as a 'simple English child' and
related a conversation with her about a New
Year's present to her parents of a quart bottle of
whisky. 'Why I had some too of course'. 'Did
you indeed, and how much?' 'Well I had a glass
to myself – Scotch it was – t'was good. I always
has it and gin sometimes – and rum – but I like
whisky best I does' – 'But doesn't it make you
tipsy!' – 'Oh...sigh! sigh! I was drunk once.' 'and
the infant became inarticulate in the merriment of
her recollections.'

In the 1890s Whistler painted several small
portraits of young girls, of which this is one of the
finest. Despite its apparent unfinished condition
with the preparatory drawing in charcoal outlining
Lizzie's dress and the grey priming of the canvas
very visible, Whistler considered it complete
enough to send to the dealers, Goupils in 1899.

Miss Rosalind Birnie Philip Standing *c.* 1897
Oil on wood. 23.4 x 13.7 cm.
Bequeathed by Miss Rosalind Philip, 1958.

This was painted in about 1897 in the drawing
room of Whistler's apartment at 110, rue du Bac,
Paris, which he had been renting for three years.
The sitter, Rosalind (1873-1958), the youngest
daughter of the sculptor John Birnie Philip, was
made Whistler's ward on the death of her elder
sister, Beatrice in 1896. She kept house for
Whistler and her mother until their deaths, also
acting as his secretary and factotum. Whistler
called her 'The Chelsea Policewoman' 'because
she always knew *everything* that was happening in
the neighbourhood'. In Whistler's correspondence
she is affectionately referred to as 'the Major' to
Whistler as 'the General' – nicknames that sprang
from Whistler's period as a military cadet at West
Point. After his death she remained strongly
attached to his memory. She jealously defended
his works and his reputation against what she
regarded as undesirable publications. She even
took legal action against Whistler's principal
biographers, Joseph and Elizabeth Robins Pennell,
informing them that he had 'more than once
expressly and definitely told me that he did not
wish his life ever to be written'.

Whistler made several drawings, a lithograph
and four oil paintings of her. This painting is a
beautiful miniature example of Whistler's late full-
length portrait style. The intimate character of this
work and of his earlier portrait of her sister, *Miss
Ethel Philip Reading* (Hunterian Art Gallery) has
some affinities with the paintings of interiors by
Edouard Vuillard (1868-1940). Whistler also
painted a large full-length portrait of Rosalind
'standing by a table covered with a white cloth on
which were silver tea or breakfast things', which
has not survived.

Green and Silver – The Great Sea   1899

Oil on wood. 17.1 x 24.8 cm. Signed with a butterfly.
Presented by Miss Rosalind Birnie Philip, 1935.

According to his biographers, the Pennells,
Whistler painted 'many small oils and
watercolours' at Pourville-sur-mer 'before the bad
weather drove him away.' This was in the
summer and early autumn of 1899. Whistler
rented a house, the Pavillon-Madeleine, in the
hamlet at the mouth of the Scie, three miles west
of Dieppe, for Rosalind Birnie Philip and her
mother. He himself stayed there 'for the
wonderful air for the healthy', with short breaks
for visits to Dordrecht, London and Paris until 26
October. Despite the fact that he was not in the
best of health Whistler managed to paint at least
ten small seapieces, the majority of them on panel.
This one he exhibited at the International Society
of Painters, Sculptors and Gravers at the Galleries
of the Royal Institute in Piccadilly in 1901 (36).

Whistler painted his first seascapes in Brittany
and near Biarritz on the Spanish border in 1861
and 1862, his last in Ireland in 1900. The earliest
paintings, such as *The Coast of Brittany*
(Wadsworth Athenaeum, Hartford, Connecticut),
are detailed and descriptive, recalling the manner
of the English genre painter James Clark Hook
(1819-1907). His experience of painting
alongside Gustave Courbet (1819-77) at Trouville
in the late autumn of 1865, coupled with his study
of Japanese prints, was probably decisive in his
decision to eliminate superfluous detail. His
seascapes from the mid 1860s are organised in a
series of flat bands of a very limited range of
colours. He was preoccupied with recreating the
atmosphere and tone of the scene, rather than with
literal representation. The group of Pourville oils
is notable for an increase in activity compared
with earlier seascapes – a more luscious use of
paint to create the effects of breaking waves and
clouds scudding rapidly across the sky.

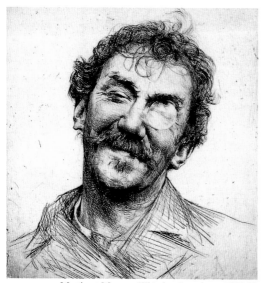

Mortimer Menpes, *Whistler*, drypoint *c.* 1886-87

Using the Collection

At least two thirds of the oil paintings by Whistler in the Hunterian Art Gallery are normally on permanent display. In addition a selection of his furniture, silver and oriental porcelain is exhibited in the Main Gallery. A selection of pastels, drawings, watercolours and prints can be seen occasionally in special exhibitions in the Print Gallery. However, the bulk of the collection is stored in the Print Room in the basement of the Gallery.

Members of the public are welcome to study material in the Print Room. However, space is limited and time must be allowed for curatorial staff to retrieve material, and plan for this in relation to other duties. Because of our small complement of staff, we are unable to offer service on demand.

We therefore ask prospective users of the Whistler Collection to write in advance of their intended visit, outlining their specific area of study, so that a suitable appointment can be made.

University Library

The archival and documentary parts of the Whistler Collection are housed in the Special Collections Department of Glasgow University Library. Students and scholars are advised to write in advance to the Keeper of Special Collections to arrange access.

1834 Birth of Whistler in Lowell, Massachusetts, 11 July.

1843 Attended drawing lessons at the Imperial Academy of Science, St. Petersburg.

1849 On the death of his father, the family returned to America.

1851 Entered West Point as cadet-at-large.

1854 Discharged from West Point for deficiency in chemistry. Learnt to etch at U.S. Coast and Geodetic Survey, Washington.

1855 Left the U.S.A. for Europe.

1856 Entered Gleyre's studio in Paris.

1857 Saw paintings by Velàzquez on exhibition in Manchester.

1858 Etching tour of Rhineland resulting in 'The French Set'. Met Fantin-Latour, Courbet and Legros.

1859 Settled in London and began 'The Thames Set' of etchings.

1860 Exhibited *At the Piano* at the Royal Academy. Joanna Hiffernan became his model and mistress.

1861 Painted in Brittany.

1862 Painted seascapes near Biarritz.

1863 Moved to Chelsea. *Succès de scandal* of *The White Girl* at the Salon des Refusés, Paris. Saw Rembrandt's prints in Amsterdam. Began collecting Japanese works of art and painting Oriental subjects.

1865 Met Albert Moore. Painted with Courbet at Trouville.

1866 Went to Valparaiso, Chile.

1867 *Symphony in White No. 3* was his first work exhibited with a musical title at the Royal Academy.

1869 Commissioned to paint the family of F.R. Leyland.

1871 First *Nocturnes* of the Thames. Painted *Arrangement in Grey and Black,* portrait of his mother.

1873 Painted Thomas Carlyle. Maud

Franklin replaced Joanna Hiffernan as model and mistress. She remained his companion for over a decade.

1874 First one-man exhibition at Flemish Gallery, Pall Mall.

1876 Decorated Leyland's dining room at 49 Princes Gate with Peacock designs.

1877 Ruskin reviewed Whistler's *Nocturne in Black and Gold: The Falling Rocket* at the Grosvenor Gallery and was sued by Whistler. Commissioned E.W. Godwin to design the White House for him at Tite Street, Chelsea.

1878 Taught lithography by Thomas Way. Awarded one farthing damages against Ruskin at the Old Bailey.

1879 Whistler declared bankrupt. Auction of Whistler's possessions. Left for Venice with a commission from The Fine Art Society for 12 etchings.

1881 Exhibition of Venice Pastels at The Fine Art Society, London.

1883 Exhibition of Venice Etchings at The Fine Art Society, London.

1884 With Mortimer Menpes and Walter Sickert in St. Ives. Exhibition of 'Notes' ≈ 'Harmonies' ≈ 'Nocturnes' at Dowdeswell, London.

1885 Delivered the 'Ten O'Clock Lecture' at Prince's Hall, London.

1886 Dowdeswell published *A Set of Twenty-Six Etchings of Venice*. Elected President of the Society of British Artists.

1887 Exhibited 50 small paintings at Galerie Georges Petit. Six lithographs, *Notes*, published by Boussod, Valadon & Cie. Sent Queen Victoria an address congratulating her on her Jubilee and 12 etchings of the naval review. The Society was granted a Royal Charter, thus becoming the Royal Society of British Artists.

1888 Resigned as President of the Royal Society of British Artists. Introduced by Monet to Stéphane Mallarmé. Married Beatrice Godwin, and honeymooned in France.

1889 'Notes' ≈ 'Harmonies' ≈ 'Nocturnes' exhibited at Wunderlich, New York. Painted and etched in Amsterdam.

1890 *The Gentle Art of Making Enemies* published. Met the American collector, C.L. Freer.

1891 Glasgow Corporation bought *Portrait of Thomas Carlyle* and the Musée du Luxembourg the *Portrait of the Painter's Mother*.

1892 Became Officier de la Légion d'Honneur. Major retrospective, *Nocturnes, Marines and Chevalet Pieces* exhibited at Goupil Gallery. Moved to 110, rue du Bac, and studio at 186, rue Notre-Dame-des-Champs, Paris.

1893 Painted in Brittany and Côtes du Nord.

1894 Du Maurier published *Trilby* caricaturing Whistler as the 'Idle Apprentice'.

1895 Painted and executed lithographs in Lyme Regis. Exhibition of lithographs at The Fine Art Society.

1896 Death of Beatrice Whistler. Visited Honfleur, Dieppe and Calais.

1897 Set up the Company of the Butterfly to sell work. Painted in Dieppe and Etrétat.

1898 Elected President of the International Society of Sculptors, Painters and Gravers. Académie Carmen set up in Paris.

1899 Painted at Pourville-sur-Mer, near Dieppe.

1900 Painted watercolours at Domburg, Holland and oils near Dublin.

1901 Visit to Marseille, Algeria and Corsica. Visited Dieppe in the summer.

1902 Visited Holland but was too ill to work.

1903 Too ill to receive doctorate of law at University of Glasgow. Died 17 July.

Publications about Whistler mirror the perception of his importance as can be seen from Robert H. Getscher and Paul G. Marks, *James McNeill Whistler and John Singer Sargent. Two Annotated Bibliographies,* New York and London, 1986 which contains informative notes on each entry. The following is a very brief guide to the most useful books and catalogues.

Life
Elizabeth Robins Pennell and Joseph Pennell, *The Life of James McNeill Whistler,* 2 vols, London & Philadelphia, 1908.
Elizabeth Robins Pennell and Joseph Pennell, *The Whistler Journal*, Philadelphia, 1921.

Glasgow University's Collection
Kate Donnelly and Nigel R. Thorp, *Whistler and Further Family,* Glasgow University Library, 1980.
Margaret F. MacDonald, *Whistler in Venice,* Hunterian Museum, University of Glasgow, 1971.
Margaret F. MacDonald, *Whistler and Mallarmé,* Hunterian Museum, University of Glasgow, 1973.
Margaret F. MacDonald, *Whistler Pastels and Related Works in the Hunterian Art Gallery,* University of Glasgow, 1984.
Denys Sutton and Martin Hopkinson, *James McNeill Whistler,* Yomiuri Shimbun, Tokyo, 1987.

Writings
James McNeill Whistler, *The Gentle Art of Making Enemies,* 2nd edition, London & New York, 1892.

Art in General
David Park Curry, *James McNeill Whistler at the Freer Gallery of Art,* Washington D.C., 1984.
Ruth E. Fine ed., 'James McNeill Whistler: a reexamination', *Studies in the History of Art,* National Gallery of Art, Washington, D.C., 1987.
Denys Sutton, *Nocturne: The Art of James McNeill Whistler,* London, 1963.
Hilary Taylor, *James McNeill Whistler,* London, 1978.

Oil Paintings
Andrew McLaren Young, Margaret F. MacDonald, Robin Spencer with Hamish Miles, *The Paintings of James McNeill Whistler,* 2 vols, New Haven and London, 1980.

Graphic Work
Ruth E. Fine, *Drawing Near: Whistler Etchings from The Zelman Collection,* Los Angeles County Museum of Art, 1984.
Susan Hobbs and Nesta R. Spink, *The Lithographs of J.M. Whistler from the Collection of Steven Louis Block,* Smithsonian Institution, Washington, D.C., 1982.
Edward G. Kennedy, *The Etched Work of Whistler...,* New York, 1910.
Edward G. Kennedy, *The Lithographs by Whistler...,* New York, 1914.
Mervyn Levy, *Whistler Lithographs. A Catalogue Raisonné,* London, 1975.
Katharine A. Lochnan, *The Etchings of James McNeill Whistler,* New Haven and London, 1984.
Margaret F. MacDonald, *Whistler, the Graphic Work...,* Thos. Agnew & Sons, London, 1976.
Howard Mansfield, *A Descriptive Catalogue of the Etchings and Drypoints of James Abbott McNeill Whistler,* Chicago, 1909.
Thomas R. Way, *Mr Whistler's Lithographs,* London, 1905.